C000090398

contents

NZ, Canada, US and UK readers
Please note that Australian cup and
spoon measurements are metric.
A conversion chart appears on page 62.

ingredients from an Asian kitchen

buk choy

daikon

choy sum

bamboo shoots

bamboo shoots tender, pale yellow, edible first-growth of the bamboo plant. Available fresh in Asian greengrocers, in season, but usually most often purchased canned; these must be drained and rinsed before use.

buk choy also known as bok choy, pak choi, chinese white cabbage or chinese chard; has a fresh, mild mustard taste. Use both stems and leaves. *Baby buk choy*, also known as pak kat farang or shanghai bok choy, is much smaller and more tender than buk choy.

chinese cooking wine also known as hao hsing or chinese rice wine; made from fermented rice, wheat, sugar and salt. Found in Asian food shops; if you can't find it, replace with mirin or sherry.

choy sum also known as pakaukeo or flowering cabbage, a member of the buk choy family; easy to identify with its long stems, light green leaves and yellow flowers, all of which are edible.

coriander also known as cilantro, pak chee or chinese parsley; bright-green-leafed herb having both pungent aroma and taste.

daikon also known as white radish; this long, white horseradish has a wonderful, sweet flavour. The flesh is white but the skin can be either white or black; available from Asian food shops.

dashi the basic fish and seaweed stock used in many Japanese dishes. Made from dried bonito (a type of tuna) flakes and kombu (kelp); instant dashi (dashi-no-moto) is available in powder, granules and liquid form from Asian food shops.

five-spice powder usually a fragrant mixture of ground cinnamon, cloves, star anise, sichuan pepper and fennel seeds. Also known as chinese five-spice.

gai lan also known as gai larn, chinese broccoli and chinese kale; green vegetable appreciated more for its stems than its coarse leaves.

galangal also known as ka or lengkaus if fresh and laos if dried and powdered; a rhizome with a hot ginger-citrusy flavour; used similarly to ginger and garlic as a seasoning or an ingredient.

ginger, pickled pink or red coloured; available, packaged, from Asian food shops. Pickled paper-thin shavings of ginger in a mixture of vinegar, sugar and natural colouring.

kaffir lime leaves also known as bai magrood; look like two glossy dark green leaves joined end to end, forming a rounded hourglass shape. A strip of fresh lime peel may be substituted for each kaffir lime leaf.

lemon grass also known as takrai, serai or serah. A tall, clumping, lemon-smelling and tasting, sharp-edged aromatic tropical grass; the white lower part of the stem is used, finely chopped.

mirin a Japanese champagne-coloured cooking wine made of glutinous rice and alcohol. Is used expressly for cooking and should not be confused with sake. A seasoned sweet mirin, manjo mirin, is also available.

mushrooms

enoki grows in clusters with long stems and small caps; has a crunchy texture and almost fruity flavour.

oyster also known as abalone; grey-white colour and shaped like a fan. Prized for their smooth texture and subtle, oyster-like flavour.

shiitake also known as chinese black, forest or golden oak mushrooms when fresh. Although cultivated, they have the earthiness and taste of wild mushrooms and are large and meaty.

gai lan

galangal

soba noodles

thai basil

noodles

dried rice stick made from rice flour and water, available flat and wide or very thin (vermicelli). Must be soaked in boiling water to soften.

egg also known as ba mee or yellow noodles; made from wheat flour and eggs, sold fresh or dried. Range in size from very fine strands to wide, spaghetti-like pieces, as thick as a shoelace.

fried crispy egg noodles that have been deep-fried then packaged for sale.

hokkien also known as stir-fry noodles; fresh wheat noodles resembling thick, yellow-brown spaghetti needing no pre-cooking before use.

rice, fresh also known as ho fun, khao pun, sen yau, pho or kway tiau. Can be purchased in strands of various widths or large sheets weighing about 500g, which are then cut into the noodle width desired. Chewy and pure white, they do not need pre-cooking before use.

rice vermicelli also known as sen mee, mei fun or bee hoon; made with rice flour. Soak the dried noodles in hot water until softened, boil them briefly then rinse with hot water before using.

soba thin, pale-brown noodle originally from Japan; made from buckwheat and varying proportions of wheat flour. Available dried and fresh, and in flavoured (green tea) varieties.

udon available fresh and dried; are broad, white wheat Japanese noodles.

sake Japan's favourite wine, made from fermented rice. If sake is unavailable, dry sherry, vermouth or brandy can be substituted.

sambal oelek also ulek or olek; Indonesian in origin, this is a salty paste made from ground chillies and vinegar.

seaweed sheet (nori) a type of dried seaweed used in Japanese cooking as a flavouring, garnish or for sushi. Sold in thin sheets, plain or toasted (yaki-nori).

shrimp paste also known as kapi, blanchan and trasi; a strong-scented, very firm preserved paste made of salted dried shrimp.

snake beans long (about 40cm), thin, round, fresh green beans; Asian in origin, with a taste similar to green or french beans. Are also known as yard-long beans because of their (pre-metric) length.

soy sauce, japanese an all-purpose low-sodium soy sauce made with more wheat content than its Chinese counterparts.

star anise a dried star-shaped pod whose seeds have an astringent aniseed flavour; commonly used to flavour stocks and marinades.

sugar, palm also known as nam tan pip, jaggery, jawa or gula melaka; made from the sap of the sugar palm tree. Light brown to black in colour and usually sold in rock-hard cakes; substitute with brown sugar, if unavailable.

tamari similar to, but thicker than, japanese soy sauce; very dark in colour with a distinctively mellow flavour. Good used as a dipping sauce or for basting.

thai basil also known as horapa; different from holy basil and sweet basil in both look and taste, having smaller leaves and purplish stems. It has a slight aniseed taste and is one of the identifying flavours of Thai food.

wombok also known as chinese cabbage, peking or napa cabbage; elongated in shape with pale green, crinkly leaves, this is the most common cabbage in South-East Asian cooking.

udon noodle soup

1.5 litres (6 cups) dashi
2 tablespoons japanese
  soy sauce
1 tablespoon mirin
2 teaspoons white sugar
2 chicken breast fillets (400g)
100g fresh shiitake mushrooms,
  sliced thinly
300g dried udon noodles
230g can sliced bamboo
  shoots, rinsed, drained
8 large spinach leaves
4 eggs
4 green onions, sliced thinly

1 Preheat oven to 220°C/200°C fan-forced.
2 Bring dashi, sauce, mirin and sugar to a boil in large saucepan; add chicken and mushrooms, return to a boil. Reduce heat; simmer, uncovered, about 10 minutes or until chicken is cooked through. Cool chicken and mushrooms in cooking liquid 10 minutes. Remove chicken from pan, slice thinly. Reserve mushroom and dashi broth.
3 Meanwhile, cook noodles in large saucepan of boiling water, uncovered, until just tender; drain. Rinse under cold water; drain.
4 Return broth to a boil. Divide noodles, chicken, bamboo shoots, spinach and hot broth with mushrooms among four 3-cup (750ml) ovenproof dishes. Make small hollows among noodles in each dish; break 1 egg into each hollow. Cook, uncovered, in oven about 10 minutes or until egg just sets.
5 Serve soup sprinkled with onion.

preparation time 10 minutes
cooking time 30 minutes
serves 4
per serving 39g total fat (8.4g saturated fat); 4761kJ (1139 cal); 121.1g carbohydrate; 85.3g protein; 27.8g fibre

prawn laksa

1kg uncooked large king prawns
⅔ cup (180g) laksa paste
3¼ cups (800ml) coconut milk
1 litre (4 cups) chicken stock
1½ cups (375ml) fish stock
1 fresh long red chilli, sliced thinly
6 kaffir lime leaves, shredded finely
250g dried rice stick noodles
3 cups (240g) bean sprouts
6 green onions, sliced thinly
1 cup (150g) roasted unsalted cashews
½ cup loosely packed fresh coriander leaves

1 Shell and devein prawns, leaving tails intact.
2 Cook paste in large heated saucepan, stirring, until fragrant. Stir in coconut milk, stocks, chilli and lime leaves; bring to a boil. Reduce heat; simmer, covered, 20 minutes.
3 Add prawns to laksa mixture; simmer, uncovered, about 5 minutes or until prawns just change in colour.
4 Meanwhile, place noodles in large heatproof bowl, cover with boiling water; stand until just tender, drain.
5 Divide noodles among serving bowls. Ladle laksa mixture over noodles; top with sprouts, onion, nuts then coriander.

preparation time 15 minutes
cooking time 30 minutes
serves 4
per serving 76.2g total fat (41.8g saturated fat); 4285kJ (1025 cal); 34.9g carbohydrate; 45.8g protein; 12.8g fibre
tip Tofu can be added to this recipe, if desired. Stir cubes of firm tofu into laksa mixture just before serving.

chiang mai noodles

vegetable oil, for deep-frying
500g fresh egg noodles
1 large brown onion (200g),
  sliced thinly
2 green onions, sliced thinly
¼ cup loosely packed fresh
  coriander leaves
¼ cup (75g) red curry paste
2 cloves garlic, crushed
¼ teaspoon ground turmeric
2 cups (500ml) water
400ml can coconut milk
500g chicken breast fillets,
  sliced thinly
¼ cup (60ml) fish sauce
1 tablespoon japanese
  soy sauce
2 tablespoons grated
  palm sugar
2 teaspoons lime juice
2 tablespoons coarsely
  chopped fresh coriander
1 fresh long red thai chilli,
  sliced thinly

1 Heat oil in wok; deep-fry about 100g of the noodles, in batches, until crisp. Drain on absorbent paper.

2 Using same heated oil, deep-fry brown onion, in batches, until browned lightly and crisp. Drain on absorbent paper. Combine fried noodles, fried onion, green onion and coriander leaves in small bowl. Discard oil from wok.

3 Place remaining noodles in large heatproof bowl, cover with boiling water; separate noodles with fork, drain.

4 Cook paste, garlic and turmeric in same cleaned wok; add the water and coconut milk, bring to a boil. Reduce heat; simmer, stirring, 2 minutes. Add chicken; cook, stirring, about 5 minutes or until chicken is cooked through. Add sauces, sugar and juice; cook, stirring, until sugar dissolves. Stir in chopped coriander.

5 Divide drained noodles among serving bowls. Spoon chicken curry mixture into each bowl; top with fried noodle mixture, sprinkle with chilli slices.

preparation time 20 minutes
cooking time 20 minutes
serves 4
per serving 34.7g total fat
(20.8g saturated fat); 3436kJ (822 cal);
80.3g carbohydrate; 43.1g protein; 7.4g fibre

soba and daikon salad

300g dried soba noodles
1 small daikon (400g), cut into matchsticks
4 green onions, sliced thinly
1 teaspoon sesame oil
100g enoki mushrooms
2 tablespoons thinly sliced pickled ginger
1 toasted seaweed sheet (yaki-nori), sliced thinly
mirin dressing
¼ cup (60ml) mirin
2 tablespoons kecap manis
1 tablespoon sake
1 clove garlic, crushed
1cm piece fresh ginger (5g), grated
1 teaspoon white sugar

1 Cook noodles in large saucepan of boiling water, uncovered, until just tender; drain. Rinse under cold water; drain.
2 Meanwhile, make mirin dressing.
3 Place noodles in large bowl with daikon, onion and half of the dressing; toss gently.
4 Heat oil in small frying pan; cook mushrooms, stirring, 2 minutes.
5 Divide noodle salad among serving plates; top with combined mushrooms, ginger and seaweed. Drizzle with remaining dressing.
mirin dressing Place ingredients in screw-top jar; shake well.

preparation time 20 minutes
cooking time 15 minutes
serves 4
per serving 2.4g total fat (0.3g saturated fat); 1292kJ (309 cal); 56.6g carbohydrate; 10.9g protein; 5.3g fibre

asian crispy noodle salad

½ medium wombok (500g), shredded finely
227g can water chestnuts, drained, sliced thinly
150g snow peas, trimmed, sliced thinly
1 large red capsicum (350g), sliced thinly
100g packet fried noodles
⅓ cup (50g) roasted unsalted cashews, chopped coarsely
1 cup loosely packed fresh coriander leaves
sesame soy dressing
1 teaspoon sesame oil
¼ cup (60ml) japanese soy sauce
1 tablespoon sweet chilli sauce
2 tablespoons lime juice

1 Make sesame soy dressing.
2 Combine wombok, water chestnuts, snow peas, capsicum and fried noodles in medium bowl.
3 Divide salad among serving bowls, sprinkle with nuts and coriander; drizzle with dressing.
sesame soy dressing Place ingredients in screw-top jar; shake well.

preparation time 15 minutes
serves 4
per serving 10.8g fat (2.2g saturated fat); 869kJ (208 cal); 19.1g carbohydrate; 8.3g protein; 6.4g fibre

crisp hot and sweet beef with noodles

750g piece beef corned silverside
1kg fresh wide rice noodles
¼ cup (60ml) peanut oil
3 cloves garlic, crushed
3 fresh small red thai chillies, sliced thinly
4 spring onions, sliced thinly
2 tablespoons fish sauce
¼ cup (65g) grated palm sugar
1 cup firmly packed fresh coriander leaves

1 Place beef, in packaging, in large saucepan, cover with cold water; bring to a boil, uncovered. Reduce heat; simmer, covered, 1½ hours. Remove from pan, discard packaging; drain beef on rack over tray for 15 minutes.

2 Meanwhile, place noodles in large heatproof bowl, cover with boiling water; separate with fork, drain.

3 Trim excess fat from beef. Using two forks, shred beef finely. Heat oil in wok; stir-fry beef, in batches, until browned all over and crisp. Drain on absorbent paper.

4 Stir-fry garlic, chilli and onion in wok until onion softens. Add sauce and sugar; stir-fry until sugar dissolves. Return beef to wok with noodles; stir-fry gently until heated through. Remove from heat; stir through coriander.

preparation time 20 minutes (plus standing time)
cooking time 1 hour 45 minutes
serves 4
per serving 23.8g total fat (6.4g saturated fat); 2905kJ (695 cal); 70.8g carbohydrate; 47.4g protein; 2.3g fibre

chilli rice noodles with buk choy

400g fresh thin rice noodles
1 tablespoon peanut oil
500g lamb mince
3 cloves garlic, crushed
2 fresh small red thai chillies, chopped finely
400g buk choy, sliced thinly
2 tablespoons tamari
1 tablespoon fish sauce
2 tablespoons kecap manis
4 green onions, sliced thinly
1 cup firmly packed thai basil leaves
3 cups (240g) bean sprouts

1 Place noodles in medium heatproof bowl, cover with boiling water; separate with fork, drain.
2 Heat oil in wok; stir-fry lamb until browned. Add garlic and chilli; stir-fry until fragrant. Add buk choy, tamari, sauce and kecap manis; stir-fry until buk choy just wilts.
3 Remove from heat; stir in onion, basil and sprouts. Serve with noodles.

preparation time 20 minutes
cooking time 15 minutes
serves 4
per serving 14.4g total fat (4.7g saturated fat); 1877kJ (449 cal); 44.5g carbohydrate; 34.3g protein; 5.3g fibre

hot-smoked trout and vermicelli salad

200g rice vermicelli noodles
400g hot-smoked trout fillets
2 trimmed celery stalks (200g),
  sliced thinly
2 lebanese cucumbers (260g),
  seeded, sliced thinly
½ cup (75g) roasted pistachios
¼ cup coarsely chopped
  fresh mint
¼ cup coarsely chopped
  thai basil
chilli dressing
⅓ cup (80ml) lime juice
1 teaspoon chilli oil
1 tablespoon sesame oil
2 tablespoons fish sauce
1 clove garlic, crushed

1 Make chilli dressing.
2 Place noodles in large heatproof bowl, cover with boiling water; stand until just tender, drain.
3 Meanwhile, discard skin and bones from fish. Flake fish into large pieces in large bowl; add noodles, celery, cucumber, nuts and herbs.
4 Drizzle dressing over salad; toss gently to combine.
chilli dressing Place ingredients in screw-top jar; shake well.

preparation time 25 minutes
cooking time 5 minutes
serves 4
per serving 20.7g total fat
(3.1g saturated fat); 1613kJ (386 cal);
16.5g carbohydrate; 31.5g protein; 4.2g fibre
tips Add more chilli oil to the dressing if you want to make the salad hotter, or use a finely chopped fresh chilli if chilli oil is unavailable. We used two hot-smoked ocean trout portions, available from supermarkets, weighing about 200g each, that were spiced with a blackening mixture of mountain pepper, aniseed myrtle, native pepperberry, salt and other flavourings before being "cooked" in hot smoking ovens. You can also use ordinary cold-smoked trout if hot-smoked trout is unavailable.

pad thai

200g dried rice stick noodles
2 cloves garlic, quartered
2 fresh small red thai chillies, chopped coarsely
2 tablespoons peanut oil
2 eggs, beaten lightly
1 cup (80g) fried shallots
125g packet fried tofu, cut into 2cm cubes
¼ cup (35g) roasted unsalted peanuts, chopped coarsely
3 cups (240g) bean sprouts
6 green onions, sliced thinly
2 tablespoons light soy sauce
1 tablespoon lime juice
2 tablespoons coarsely chopped fresh coriander

1 Place noodles in large heatproof bowl, cover with boiling water; stand until just tender, drain.

2 Meanwhile, using mortar and pestle, crush garlic and chilli to a paste.

3 Heat 2 teaspoons of the oil in wok. Pour egg into wok; cook over medium heat, tilting pan, until almost set. Remove omelette from wok; roll tightly, slice thinly.

4 Heat remaining oil in wok, stir-fry garlic paste and shallots until fragrant. Add tofu; stir-fry 1 minute. Add half the nuts, half the sprouts and half the onion; stir-fry until spouts are just wilted.

5 Add noodles, sauce and juice; stir-fry until hot. Remove from heat; sprinkle omelette, coriander and remaining nuts, sprouts and onion over pad thai.

preparation time 20 minutes
cooking time 10 minutes
serves 4
per serving 19.6g total fat (3.4g saturated fat); 1246kJ (298 cal); 15.1g carbohydrate; 13.4g protein; 4.3g fibre

five-spice tofu with egg noodles and lemon chilli sauce

½ cup (125ml) sweet chilli sauce
2 teaspoons finely grated lemon rind
¼ cup (60ml) lemon juice
440g fresh egg noodles
⅓ cup (50g) plain flour
2 teaspoons five-spice powder
300g firm tofu, cut into 2cm pieces
1 tablespoon olive oil
1 large brown onion (200g), chopped coarsely
3 cloves garlic, sliced thinly
1 small yellow capsicum (150g), sliced thinly
300g sugar snap peas, trimmed

1 Combine sauce, rind and juice in small saucepan; bring to a boil. Remove from heat.
2 Place noodles in large heatproof bowl, cover with boiling water; separate with fork, drain.
3 Combine flour and five-spice in medium bowl, add tofu; toss to coat tofu in flour mixture.
4 Heat half the oil in wok; cook tofu, in batches, until browned all over.
5 Heat remaining oil in wok; stir-fry onion, garlic and capsicum until onion softens. Add noodles, peas and half the lemon chilli sauce; stir-fry until peas are just tender.
6 Serve noodles with tofu; drizzle with remaining lemon chilli sauce.

preparation time 15 minutes
cooking time 25 minutes
serves 4
per serving 12.2g total fat (1.8g saturated fat); 2241kJ (536 cal); 80.3g carbohydrate; 24.6g protein; 8.5g fibre

lemon grass chicken
with chilli dipping sauce

200g rice vermicelli noodles
2 tablespoons peanut oil
600g chicken thigh fillets,
    sliced thinly
2 x 10cm sticks fresh lemon
    grass (40g), chopped finely
1 clove garlic, crushed
1 tablespoon fish sauce
2 cups (120g) shredded
    iceberg lettuce
1 medium carrot (120g),
    grated coarsely
1 lebanese cucumber (130g),
    halved, seeded, sliced thinly
¼ cup (35g) roasted peanuts,
    chopped coarsely
1 red radish (35g), grated finely
chilli dipping sauce
⅓ cup (75g) white sugar
½ cup (125ml) water
1 tablespoon white vinegar
1 fresh small red thai chilli,
    chopped finely

1 Place noodles in medium heatproof bowl, cover with boiling water. Stand until tender; drain. Rinse under cold water; drain.

2 Meanwhile, make chilli dipping sauce

3 Heat 1 tablespoon of the oil in wok; stir-fry chicken, in batches, until browned and cooked through. Return chicken to wok with remaining oil, lemon grass and garlic. Cook about 1 minute or until fragrant. Add fish sauce; stir-fry to coat chicken in sauce.

4 Divide noodles among serving bowls. Top with lettuce, carrot, cucumber and chicken mixture. Sprinkle with nuts and radish. Serve with chilli dipping sauce.

chilli dipping sauce Combine sugar and water in small saucepan. Stir over low heat until sugar dissolves; bring to a boil. Reduce heat; simmer, uncovered, about 2 minutes or until sauce thickens slightly. Remove from heat; stir in vinegar and chilli.

preparation time 20 minutes
cooking time 10 minutes
serves 4
per serving 24.4g total fat
(5.4g saturated fat); 2157kJ (516 cal);
46.5g carbohydrate; 32.3g protein; 2.9g fibre

char kway teow

450g fresh wide rice noodles
250g uncooked medium prawns
250g squid hoods
⅓ cup (80ml) peanut oil
250g firm white fish fillets,
   skinned, cut into 3cm pieces
2 cloves garlic, crushed
2 fresh small red thai chillies,
   chopped finely
4cm piece fresh ginger
   (20g), grated
2 eggs, beaten lightly
5 green onions, sliced thinly
2 cups (160g) bean sprouts
120g dried chinese sausage,
   sliced thinly
2 tablespoons dark soy sauce
1 tablespoon light soy sauce
1 tablespoon kecap manis

1 Place noodles in large heatproof bowl, cover with boiling water; separate with fork, drain.

2 Shell and devein prawns, leaving tails intact. Cut squid down centre to open out; score inside in diagonal pattern then cut into 2cm-wide strips.

3 Heat 1 tablespoon of the oil in wok; stir-fry fish and squid, in batches, until browned lightly. Place in large bowl; cover to keep warm.

4 Heat another tablespoon of the oil in wok; stir-fry prawns, garlic, chilli and ginger until prawns just change colour. Add to bowl with fish and squid; cover to keep warm.

5 Heat remaining oil in wok; stir-fry egg, onion and sprouts until egg is just set. Slide egg mixture onto plate; cover to keep warm.

6 Stir-fry sausage in wok until crisp; drain. Return sausage to wok with seafood, egg mixture, sauces, kecap manis and noodles; stir-fry until hot.

preparation time 20 minutes
cooking time 15 minutes
serves 4
per serving 29.9g total fat
(6.9g saturated fat); 2291kJ (548 cal);
27g carbohydrate; 41.1g protein; 3.3g fibre
tip Dried chinese sausages, also called lop chong, are usually made from pork, but can also be made with duck liver or beef. Red-brown in colour and sweet-spicy in flavour, the 12cm dried links are sold, several strung together, in Asian food stores.

hokkien mee with beef

300g hokkien noodles
1 tablespoon peanut oil
700g beef rump steak, sliced thinly
1 medium brown onion (150g), sliced thinly
3cm piece fresh ginger (15g), grated
2 cloves garlic, crushed
2 fresh small red thai chillies, sliced thinly
1 small red capsicum (150g), sliced thinly
1 small green capsicum (150g), sliced thinly
200g button mushrooms, quartered
2 tablespoons hoisin sauce
1 tablespoon dark soy sauce

1 Place noodles in medium heatproof bowl, cover with boiling water; separate with fork, drain.
2 Heat half the oil in wok; stir-fry beef, in batches, until browned.
3 Heat remaining oil in wok; stir-fry onion until soft. Add ginger, garlic and chilli; stir-fry until fragrant. Add capsicums and mushrooms; stir-fry until tender.
4 Return beef to wok with noodles and sauces; stir-fry until hot.

preparation time 15 minutes
cooking time 15 minutes
serves 4
per serving 17.4g total fat (6.2g saturated fat); 1927kJ (461 cal); 27.2g carbohydrate; 46.1g protein; 5.3g fibre

beef chow mein

1 tablespoon vegetable oil
500g beef mince
1 medium brown onion (150g), chopped finely
2 cloves garlic, crushed
1 tablespoon curry powder
1 large carrot (180g), chopped finely
2 trimmed celery stalks (200g), sliced thinly
150g button mushrooms, sliced thinly
1 cup (250ml) chicken stock
⅓ cup (80ml) oyster sauce
2 tablespoons dark soy sauce
440g fresh thin egg noodles
½ cup (60g) frozen peas
½ small wombok (350g), shredded coarsely

1 Heat oil in wok; stir-fry beef, onion and garlic until beef is browned. Add curry powder; stir-fry about 1 minute or until fragrant. Add carrot, celery and mushrooms; stir-fry until vegetables soften.
2 Add stock, sauces and noodles; stir-fry 2 minutes. Add peas and wombok; stir-fry until wombok just wilts.

preparation time 30 minutes
cooking time 20 minutes
serves 4
per serving 15.7g total fat (4.6g saturated fat); 2571kJ (615 cal); 70.6g carbohydrate; 42.3g protein; 8.4g fibre

balinese chilli lamb and fried noodles

600g hokkien noodles
1 tablespoon sambal oelek
1 tablespoon dark soy sauce
1 tablespoon fish sauce
2 cloves garlic, crushed
750g lamb backstraps,
    sliced thinly
¼ cup (60ml) peanut oil
⅓ cup (55g) coarsely chopped
    brazil nuts
⅔ cup (160ml) beef stock
2 tablespoons oyster sauce
2 tablespoons lime juice
2 teaspoons brown sugar
150g sugar snap peas, trimmed
⅓ cup finely chopped fresh mint
2 fresh small red thai chillies,
    chopped finely

1 Place noodles in large heatproof bowl, cover with boiling water; separate with fork, drain.
2 Combine sambal, soy sauce, fish sauce and garlic in large bowl with lamb.
3 Heat half a teaspoon of oil in wok; stir-fry nuts until browned lightly. Remove from wok.
4 Heat 2 tablespoons of remaining oil in wok; stir-fry lamb, in batches, until browned.
5 Heat remaining oil in wok; stir-fry noodles until browned lightly.
6 Add stock, oyster sauce, juice and sugar to wok; simmer about 3 minutes or until sauce thickens slightly.
7 Return lamb to wok with peas; stir-fry until hot. Serve noodles topped with lamb mixture and sprinkled with nuts, mint and chilli.

preparation time 15 minutes
cooking time 10 minutes
serves 4
per serving 40.5g total fat
(12.1g saturated fat); 3164kJ (757 cal);
45.4g carbohydrate; 50.2g protein; 5.4g fibre

chilli-chicken stir-fry with asian greens

2½ cups (500g) jasmine rice
1 tablespoon sesame oil
4 chicken breast fillets (800g), sliced thinly
2 cloves garlic, crushed
1 large red capsicum (350g), sliced thinly
⅓ cup (100g) thai chilli jam
2 tablespoons sweet chilli sauce
¼ cup (60ml) chicken stock
500g baby buk choy, halved lengthways
225g can water chestnuts, drained, halved
4 green onions, sliced thinly
1 tablespoon sesame seeds, toasted

1 Cook rice in large saucepan of boiling water, uncovered, until just tender; drain. Cover to keep warm.

2 Meanwhile, heat half the oil in wok; stir-fry chicken, in batches, until cooked through. Return chicken to wok with garlic, capsicum, jam, sauce and stock; stir-fry about 2 minutes or until sauce thickens slightly. Remove from wok.

3 Heat remaining oil in cleaned wok; stir-fry buk choy, chestnuts and onion until buk choy just wilts. Divide buk choy mixture among serving plates; top with chilli chicken, sprinkle with sesame seeds. Serve with rice.

preparation time 10 minutes
cooking time 15 minutes
serves 4
per serving 13.7g total fat (2.7g saturated fat); 3490kJ (835 cal); 115.9g carbohydrate; 57.6g protein; 5.4g fibre

aromatic vietnamese beef stir-fry

2 tablespoons peanut oil
800g beef strips
1 medium brown onion (150g), chopped finely
3 cloves garlic, crushed
1 fresh long red chilli, chopped finely
10cm stick fresh lemon grass (20g), chopped finely
1 star anise
1 cinnamon stick
4 cardamom pods, bruised
350g snake beans, cut in 4cm lengths
2 tablespoons ground bean sauce
2 tablespoons fish sauce
½ cup coarsely chopped fresh coriander
½ cup (40g) roasted almond flakes

1 Heat half the oil in wok; stir-fry beef, in batches, until browned.
Cover to keep warm.
2 Heat remaining oil in wok; stir-fry onion until soft. Add garlic, chilli,
lemon grass, star anise, cinnamon, cardamom and beans; stir-fry until
beans are tender. Discard star anise, cinnamon and cardamom. Return
beef to wok with sauces; stir-fry until heated through. Remove from heat;
stir in coriander and nuts.

preparation time 15 minutes
cooking time 20 minutes
serves 4
per serving 27.2g total fat (7.1g saturated fat); 2011kJ (481 cal);
7.4g carbohydrate; 49.6g protein; 4.9g fibre

nasi goreng

1 small brown onion (80g),
  chopped coarsely
2 cloves garlic, quartered
5cm piece fresh ginger (25g),
  chopped coarsely
2 fresh long red chillies,
  chopped coarsely
1 tablespoon peanut oil
4 eggs, beaten lightly
150g oyster mushrooms,
  chopped coarsely
1 medium green capsicum
  (200g), chopped coarsely
1 medium red capsicum (200g),
  chopped coarsely
200g fresh baby corn,
  chopped coarsely
4 cups cooked jasmine rice
1 cup (80g) bean sprouts
3 green onions, sliced thinly
2 tablespoons japanese
  soy sauce
1 tablespoon kecap manis

1 Blend or process brown onion, garlic, ginger and chilli until almost smooth.

2 Heat 1 teaspoon of the oil in wok; add half the egg, swirl wok to make thin omelette. Cook, uncovered, until egg is just set. Remove from wok; cut into thick strips. Repeat process with another 1 teaspoon of the oil and remaining egg.

3 Heat remaining oil in wok; stir-fry onion mixture until fragrant. Add mushrooms, capsicums and corn; stir-fry until tender.

4 Add rice, sprouts, green onion, sauce and kecap manis; stir-fry until heated through.

5 Serve topped with omelette strips.

preparation time 20 minutes
cooking time 15 minutes
serves 4
per serving 11.2g total fat (2.5g saturated fat); 1843kJ (441 cal); 66.8g carbohydrate; 17.6g protein; 7.2g fibre
tip You need to cook about 2 cups of jasmine rice the day before you make this recipe. Spread the rice out in a thin layer on a tray, cover, and refrigerate overnight.

asian greens stir-fry with kaffir lime rice

1 litre (4 cups) cold water
2 cups (400g) jasmine rice
4 fresh kaffir lime leaves, shredded
4cm piece fresh ginger (20g), chopped coarsely
2 fresh long red chillies, chopped coarsely
1 tablespoon sesame oil
1 large brown onion (200g), sliced thickly
200g green beans, trimmed
300g baby buk choy, quartered lengthways
100g snow peas, trimmed
150g oyster mushrooms, halved
100g enoki mushrooms, trimmed
⅓ cup (80ml) lime juice
2 tablespoons japanese soy sauce
¼ cup coarsely chopped fresh coriander

1 Combine the water, rice, lime leaves, ginger and chilli in large saucepan with a tight-fitting lid; bring to a boil. Reduce heat, cook, covered, about 12 minutes or until all water is absorbed and rice is cooked. Do not remove lid or stir rice during cooking time. Remove from heat; stand, covered, 10 minutes.
2 Meanwhile, heat half the oil in wok; stir-fry onion until just softened. Add beans; stir-fry until just tender. Add buk choy, snow peas and mushrooms; stir-fry until buk choy just wilts. Add juice, sauce, coriander and remaining oil; stir-fry to combine. Serve stir-fry with rice.

preparation time 15 minutes
cooking time 20 minutes
serves 4
per serving 5.7g total fat (0.8g saturated fat); 1889kJ (452 cal); 85.7g carbohydrate; 12.9g protein; 7g fibre

mongolian lamb stir-fry

1½ cups (300g) white long-grain rice
2 tablespoons peanut oil
600g lamb strips
2 cloves garlic, crushed
1cm piece fresh ginger (5g), grated
1 medium brown onion (150g), sliced thickly
1 medium red capsicum (200g), sliced thickly
230g can bamboo shoots, rinsed, drained
¼ cup (60ml) japanese soy sauce
1 tablespoon black bean sauce
1 tablespoon cornflour
2 tablespoons rice wine vinegar
6 green onions, cut into 5cm lengths

1 Cook rice in large saucepan of boiling water, uncovered, until just tender; drain. Cover to keep warm.

2 Meanwhile, heat half the oil in wok; stir-fry lamb, in batches, until browned all over.

3 Heat remaining oil in wok; stir-fry garlic, ginger and brown onion until onion softens. Add capsicum and bamboo shoots; stir-fry until vegetables are just tender. Return lamb to wok with sauces and blended cornflour and vinegar; stir-fry until sauce boils and thickens slightly. Remove from heat; stir in green onion. Serve stir-fry with rice.

preparation time 15 minutes
cooking time 20 minutes
serves 4
per serving 23.2g total fat (7.8g saturated fat); 2709kJ (648 cal); 68.7g carbohydrate; 40.4g protein; 3.5g fibre

pork and lemon grass stir-fry

1 tablespoon peanut oil
10cm stick fresh lemon grass (20g), chopped finely
2 fresh small red thai chillies, chopped finely
2 teaspoons finely grated fresh galangal
2 cloves garlic, crushed
500g pork mince
1 tablespoon red curry paste
100g green beans, trimmed, chopped coarsely
2 tablespoons fish sauce
2 tablespoons lime juice
1 tablespoon grated palm sugar
1 small red onion (100g), sliced thinly
2 green onions, sliced thinly
¼ cup loosely packed thai basil leaves
¼ cup firmly packed fresh coriander leaves
¼ cup (35g) roasted peanuts, chopped coarsely
4 large iceberg lettuce leaves

1 Heat oil in wok; stir-fry lemon grass, chilli, galangal and garlic until fragrant. Add pork; stir-fry about 5 minutes or until browned. Add paste; stir-fry until fragrant.
2 Add beans, sauce, juice and sugar to wok; stir-fry about 5 minutes or until beans are just tender. Remove from heat; stir in onions, herbs and half the nuts.
3 Divide lettuce leaves among serving plates; spoon pork mixture into lettuce leaves, sprinkle with remaining nuts.

preparation time 10 minutes
cooking time 12 minutes
serves 4
per serving 19.5g total fat (4.9g saturated fat); 1350kJ (323 cal); 7.2g carbohydrate; 29.8g protein; 3.7g fibre

thai prawn stir-fry

5 dried long red chillies
1.5kg uncooked medium prawns
2 tablespoons coarsely chopped fresh galangal
10cm stick fresh lemon grass (20g), chopped coarsely
2 tablespoons coarsely chopped coriander root and stem mixture
2 cloves garlic, crushed
1 teaspoon shrimp paste
2 tablespoons vegetable oil
8 fresh kaffir lime leaves, torn
2 tablespoons water
1 tablespoon fish sauce
1 teaspoon caster sugar
1 medium green apple (150g), unpeeled, cut into matchsticks
2 shallots (50g), sliced thinly
½ cup firmly packed fresh coriander leaves
2 fresh long red chillies, sliced thinly

1 Place dried chillies in small heatproof jug, cover with boiling water; stand 15 minutes, drain.
2 Shell and devein prawns, leaving tails intact.
3 Blend or process soaked chillies, galangal, lemon grass, coriander root and stem mixture, garlic, paste, half the oil and half the lime leaf until mixture forms a paste.
4 Transfer paste mixture to large bowl, add prawns; mix well.
5 Heat remaining oil in wok; stir-fry prawn mixture with remaining lime leaf until prawns are changed in colour. Add the water, sauce and sugar; stir-fry 1 minute. Remove from heat; toss apple, shallot, coriander leaves and fresh chilli into stir-fry.

preparation time 10 minutes (plus standing time)
cooking time 15 minutes
serves 4
per serving 10.6g total fat (1.4g saturated fat); 1183kJ (283 cal); 6.1g carbohydrate; 40g protein; 1.5g fibre
tip When purchasing coriander, make sure you buy stems that also have the root attached for this recipe. Wash well before using.

twice-fried sichuan beef

600g piece beef eye fillet,
   sliced thinly
2 tablespoons dry sherry
2 tablespoons japanese
   soy sauce
1 teaspoon brown sugar
½ cup (75g) cornflour
1½ cups (300g) jasmine rice
vegetable oil, for deep-frying
2 teaspoons sesame oil
1 clove garlic, crushed
1 fresh small red thai chilli,
   chopped finely
1 medium brown onion (150g),
   sliced thickly
1 medium carrot (120g), halved,
   sliced thinly
1 small red capsicum (150g),
   sliced thinly
500g gai lan, chopped coarsely
1 tablespoon cracked
   sichuan peppercorns
2 tablespoons oyster sauce
¼ cup (60ml) japanese
   soy sauce, extra
½ cup (125ml) beef stock
2 teaspoons brown sugar, extra

1 Combine beef, sherry, soy sauce and sugar in medium bowl. Stand 10 minutes; drain. Toss beef in cornflour; shake off excess.

2 Meanwhile, cook rice in large saucepan of boiling water, uncovered, until just tender; drain. Cover to keep warm.

3 Heat vegetable oil in wok; deep-fry beef, in batches, until crisp. Drain on absorbent paper. Reserve oil for another use.

4 Heat sesame oil in cleaned wok; stir-fry garlic, chilli and onion until onion softens. Add carrot and capsicum; stir-fry until just tender. Add gai lan; stir-fry until just wilted. Add beef, peppercorns, oyster sauce, extra soy sauce, stock and extra sugar; stir-fry until heated through. Serve beef and vegetables with rice.

preparation time 20 minutes
cooking time 25 minutes
serves 4
per serving 18.8g total fat
(4.7g saturated fat); 2959kJ (768 cal);
87.3g carbohydrate; 41.3g protein; 4.5g fibre
tip It is easier to slice beef thinly if it is
partially frozen.

peanut chilli beef with choy sum

700g beef strips
½ cup (140g) crunchy peanut butter
¼ cup (75g) sambal oelek
¼ cup (60ml) kecap manis
2 tablespoons peanut oil
2 medium white onions (300g), cut into 8 wedges
½ small wombok (350g), shredded coarsely
400g choy sum, chopped coarsely

1 Place beef in medium bowl with half the peanut butter, 2 teaspoons of the sambal and 2 teaspoons of the kecap manis; rub peanut butter mixture into beef.
2 Combine remaining peanut butter, sambal and kecap manis in small jug.
3 Heat half the oil in wok; stir-fry beef, in batches, until cooked as desired. Cover to keep warm.
4 Heat remaining oil in wok; stir-fry onion and wombok, in batches, until browned lightly. Return onion and wombok to wok with choy sum; stir-fry to combine, then pour reserved peanut butter mixture into wok. Stir-fry until choy sum just wilts and mixture is hot.
5 Serve vegetable mixture topped with beef.

preparation time 10 minutes
cooking time 15 minutes
serves 4
per serving 37.7g total fat (9g saturated fat); 2541kJ (608 cal); 13.8g carbohydrate; 50.7g protein; 7.2g fibre

capsicum, chilli and hoisin chicken stir-fry

800g chicken breast fillets,
    sliced thinly
2 cloves garlic, crushed
1½ teaspoons five-spice
    powder
10cm stick fresh lemon grass
    (20g), chopped finely
2cm piece fresh ginger
    (10g), grated
2 tablespoons peanut oil
1 medium brown onion (150g),
    sliced thinly
1 fresh long red thai chilli,
    chopped finely
1 medium red capsicum (200g),
    sliced thickly
⅓ cup (80ml) hoisin sauce
2 teaspoons finely grated
    lemon rind
1 tablespoon lemon juice
½ cup coarsely chopped
    fresh coriander
2 tablespoons fried shallots
1 green onion, sliced thinly

1 Combine chicken with half the garlic, 1 teaspoon of the five-spice and all of the lemon grass and ginger in large bowl. Cover, refrigerate 1 hour.

2 Heat half the oil in wok; stir-fry brown onion, chilli, capsicum and remaining garlic until onion softens. Remove from wok.

3 Heat remaining oil in wok; stir-fry chicken, in batches, until cooked.

4 Return onion mixture and chicken to wok with sauce, rind, juice and remaining five-spice; stir-fry until sauce thickens slightly. Remove from heat, toss through coriander; sprinkle with shallots and green onion.

preparation time 15 minutes
(plus refrigeration time)
cooking time 15 minutes
serves 4
per serving 15.4g total fat
(3.1g saturated fat); 1601kJ (383 cal);
12.1g carbohydrate; 47.2g protein; 3.9g fibre
tip Fried shallots are usually served as a condiment on the table or sprinkled over cooked dishes. They can be purchased packaged in jars or cellophane bags at all Asian grocery stores; once opened, they will keep for months if stored tightly sealed. You can make your own by frying thinly sliced shallots until crisp and golden brown.

peppercorn beef

2 tablespoons japanese soy sauce
3cm piece fresh ginger (15g), grated
2 cloves garlic, crushed
2 teaspoons cornflour
1 teaspoon sesame oil
800g beef rump steak, sliced thinly
2 teaspoons pepper medley
¼ teaspoon sichuan peppercorns
2 tablespoons peanut oil
1 medium brown onion (150g), sliced thinly
150g snake beans, chopped coarsely
2 tablespoons chinese cooking wine
½ cup (125ml) water
2 tablespoons oyster sauce
4 green onions, sliced thickly

1 Combine soy sauce, ginger, garlic, cornflour and sesame oil in large bowl; add beef, mix well. Cover; refrigerate 1 hour.
2 Meanwhile, using mortar and pestle, crush pepper medley and sichuan peppercorns finely.
3 Heat half the peanut oil in wok; stir-fry beef, in batches, until browned.
4 Heat remaining oil in wok; stir-fry brown onion, beans and pepper mixture until onion is tender. Return beef to wok with cooking wine, the water and oyster sauce; bring to a boil. Stir-fry until beans are tender. Remove from heat; stir in green onion.

preparation time 20 minutes (plus refrigeration time)
cooking time 20 minutes
serves 4
per serving 24g total fat (7.8g saturated fat); 1889kJ (452 cal); 7.6g carbohydrate; 47.8g protein; 2.1g fibre
tip Pepper medley is a mixture of black, white, green and pink peppercorns, coriander seeds and allspice, and is sold in grinders in supermarkets. You can use your own blend of various peppercorns, if you prefer.

crisp twice-fried lamb with thai basil

⅓ cup (80ml) sweet chilli sauce
¼ cup (60ml) oyster sauce
2 tablespoons light soy sauce
800g lamb strips
¾ cup (110g) plain flour
vegetable oil, for deep-frying
1 tablespoon vegetable oil, extra
1 small brown onion (80g), sliced thinly
2 cloves garlic, sliced thinly
250g sugar snap peas, trimmed
2 cups (160g) bean sprouts
1 cup loosely packed thai basil leaves

1 Combine sauces in small jug; pour two-thirds of the sauce mixture into medium bowl with lamb, mix well. Drain lamb, discard liquid.
2 Coat lamb in flour; shake off excess. Heat oil in wok; deep-fry lamb, in batches, until browned. Drain.
3 Heat extra oil in cleaned wok; stir-fry onion and garlic until onion softens. Add peas and remaining sauce mixture; stir-fry until peas are almost tender.
4 Return lamb to wok; stir-fry until hot. Remove from heat; stir in sprouts and basil.

preparation time 15 minutes
cooking time 20 minutes
serves 4
per serving 34.5g total fat (10.2g saturated fat); 2713kJ (649 cal); 32.4g carbohydrate; 49.6g protein; 5.4g fibre

sticky pork with vegies

1 tablespoon honey
2 tablespoons light soy sauce
2 tablespoons brown sugar
1 teaspoon five-spice powder
1 teaspoon hot chilli powder
3 cloves garlic, crushed
1 teaspoon sesame oil
750g pork neck, cut into 3cm cubes
2 tablespoons peanut oil
½ cup (70g) raw peanuts, chopped coarsely
1 medium carrot (120g), cut into matchsticks
150g snow peas, trimmed, sliced thinly lengthways
2 tablespoons orange juice
3 kaffir lime leaves, shredded
4 green onions, sliced thinly

1 Combine honey, sauce, sugar, five-spice, chilli, garlic and sesame oil in large bowl; add pork, turn to coat in marinade. Cover; refrigerate 3 hours or overnight.
2 Heat half the peanut oil in wok; stir-fry nuts until browned. Drain.
3 Heat remaining oil in wok. Add pork; stir-fry, in batches, until browned. Return pork to wok with carrot; stir-fry until pork is cooked.
4 Add snow peas, juice and lime leaves; stir-fry until snow peas are tender. Remove from heat; toss in onion and nuts.

preparation time 15 minutes (plus refrigeration time)
cooking time 25 minutes
serves 4
per serving 33.7g total fat (8.1g saturated fat); 2366kJ (566 cal); 18.5g carbohydrate; 46.4g protein; 3.8g fibre

glossary

bean sprouts also known as bean shoots; tender new growths of assorted beans and seeds germinated for consumption as sprouts.

capsicum also known as pepper or bell pepper.

cardamom a spice native to India; can be purchased in pod, seed or ground form. Has a distinctive aromatic, sweetly rich flavour.

chilli always use rubber gloves when seeding and chopping fresh chillies as they can burn your skin.

  long red available both fresh and dried; a generic term used for any long, thin moderately-hot chilli.

  powder the Asian variety is the hottest, made from dried ground thai chillies.

  thai red also known as "scuds"; tiny, very hot and bright red in colour.

cinnamon available whole (called sticks or quills) or ground into powder.

coconut milk the diluted liquid from the second pressing of the white flesh of a mature coconut (the first pressing produces coconut cream).

cornflour also known as cornstarch.

curry powder a blend of some of the following ground spices: dried chilli, cinnamon, coriander, cumin, fennel, fenugreek, mace, cardamom and turmeric.

eggs some recipes in this book call for raw or barely cooked eggs; exercise caution if there's a salmonella problem in your community.

flour, plain also known as all-purpose flour.

ginger, fresh also known as green or root ginger; the thick gnarled root of a tropical plant. Keep frozen or refrigerated, peeled and covered with dry sherry, in an airtight container. Fresh ginger cannot be substituted with powdered ginger.

mince also known as ground meat.

oil

  chilli oil that has been infused with chillies.

  olive made from ripened olives. *Extra virgin* and *virgin* are the first and second press, respectively, of the olives and are therefore considered the best; the *extra light* or *light* name on other types refers to taste not fat levels.

  peanut pressed from ground peanuts; the most commonly used oil in Asian cooking because of its high smoke point (able to handle high heat without burning).

  sesame made from roasted, crushed, white sesame seeds; a flavouring rather than a cooking medium.

  vegetable any of a number of oils sourced from plants rather than animal fats.

onion

  green also known as scallion or, incorrectly, shallot; an immature onion picked before the bulb has formed, having a long, bright-green edible stalk.

  shallots also called french shallots, golden shallots or eschalots. Small, elongated, brown-skinned members of the onion family. *Fried shallots* can be purchased packaged in jars or cellophane bags at all Asian grocery stores; once opened, they keep for months if stored tightly sealed. Make your own by frying thinly sliced shallots until crisp and golden-brown.

  spring has crisp, narrow green-leafed tops and a round sweet white bulb larger than green onions.

red curry paste ingredients include red chilli, garlic, shallot, lemon grass, salt, galangal, shrimp paste, kaffir lime peel, cumin, coriander and paprika. It is milder than the hotter thai green curry paste.

sherry fortified wine that is consumed as an aperitif or used in cooking.

sauces

  bean a mixture of soy beans, flour, salt, sugar and water.

  black bean an Asian sauce made from spices, salted and fermented soy beans and wheat flour.

fish called naam pla or nuoc naam. Made from pulverised salted fermented fish (most often anchovies); has a pungent smell and strong taste. Available in varying degrees of intensity, so use according to your taste.

hoisin a thick, sweet and spicy Chinese barbecue sauce made from salted fermented soybeans, onions and garlic.

oyster Asian in origin, this thick, richly-flavoured brown sauce is made from oysters and their brine, cooked with salt and soy sauce, and thickened with starches.

soy also known as sieu; made from fermented soybeans. Several variations are available from Asian food stores and supermarkets; we use Japanese soy sauce unless indicated otherwise. *Dark soy* is deep brown and almost black in colour; rich, with a thicker consistency than other types. Pungent, but not particularly salty; it is good for marinating. *Kecap manis* is a dark, thick sweet soy sauce with palm sugar or molasses added. *Light soy* is fairly thin and, while paler than the others, the saltiest tasting; used in dishes in which the natural colour of the ingredients is to be maintained. Not to be confused with salt-reduced or low-sodium soy sauces.

sweet chilli comparatively mild, fairly sticky and runny sauce made from red chillies, sugar, garlic and white vinegar; used in Thai cooking and as a condiment.

teriyaki either home-made or commercially bottled, this Japanese sauce, made from soy sauce, mirin, sugar, ginger and other spices, imparts a distinctive glaze when brushed over grilled meat or poultry.

sichuan peppercorns also known as szechuan or chinese pepper, native to the Sichuan province of China; a mildly-hot spice. Although it is not related to the peppercorn family, small, red-brown aromatic sichuan berries look like black peppercorns and have a distinctive peppery-lemon flavour and aroma.

snow peas also called mange tout; a variety of garden pea, eaten pod and all (although you may need to string them).

spinach also known as english spinach and, incorrectly, silver beet.

sugar snap peas also known as honey snap peas; fresh small pea that can be eaten whole, pod and all.

sugar
brown soft, finely granulated sugar retaining molasses for its characteristic colour and flavour.

caster also known as superfine or finely granulated table sugar.

white a coarse, granulated table sugar, also known as crystal sugar.

thai chilli jam a combination of garlic, shallots, chilli, tomato paste, fish sauce, galangal, spices and shrimp paste; it is sold under various names, and can be found in the Asian food section of the supermarket.

tofu, fried packaged pieces of deep-fried soft bean curd; the surface is brown and crunchy and the inside almost totally dried out. Add to stir-fries and soups at the last minute so they don't soak up too much liquid.

turmeric also known as kamin; is a rhizome related to galangal and ginger. Must be grated or pounded to release its somewhat acrid aroma and pungent flavour. Known for the golden colour it imparts, fresh turmeric can be substituted with the more common dried powder.

water chestnuts resemble true chestnuts in appearance, hence the English name. Small brown tubers with a crisp, crunchy, white, nutty-tasting flesh. Best eaten fresh, however, canned water chestnuts are more easily obtained and can be kept for about a month in the fridge, once opened.

conversion chart

MEASURES

One Australian metric measuring cup holds approximately 250ml, one Australian metric tablespoon holds 20ml, one Australian metric teaspoon holds 5ml.

The difference between one country's measuring cups and another's is within a 2- or 3-teaspoon variance, and will not affect your cooking results. North America, New Zealand and the United Kingdom use a 15ml tablespoon. All cup and spoon measurements are level. The most accurate way of measuring dry ingredients is to weigh them. When measuring liquids, use a clear glass or plastic jug with metric markings.

We use large eggs with an average weight of 60g.

DRY MEASURES

METRIC	IMPERIAL
15g	½oz
30g	1oz
60g	2oz
90g	3oz
125g	4oz (¼lb)
155g	5oz
185g	6oz
220g	7oz
250g	8oz (½lb)
280g	9oz
315g	10oz
345g	11oz
375g	12oz (¾lb)
410g	13oz
440g	14oz
470g	15oz
500g	16oz (1lb)
750g	24oz (1½lb)
1kg	32oz (2lb)

LIQUID MEASURES

METRIC	IMPERIAL
30ml	1 fluid oz
60ml	2 fluid oz
100ml	3 fluid oz
125ml	4 fluid oz
150ml	5 fluid oz (¼ pint/1 gill)
190ml	6 fluid oz
250ml	8 fluid oz
300ml	10 fluid oz (½ pint)
500ml	16 fluid oz
600ml	20 fluid oz (1 pint)
1000ml (1 litre)	1¾ pints

LENGTH MEASURES

METRIC	IMPERIAL
3mm	⅛in
6mm	¼in
1cm	½in
2cm	¾in
2.5cm	1in
5cm	2in
6cm	2½in
8cm	3in
10cm	4in
13cm	5in
15cm	6in
18cm	7in
20cm	8in
23cm	9in
25cm	10in
28cm	11in
30cm	12in (1ft)

OVEN TEMPERATURES

These oven temperatures are only a guide for conventional ovens. For fan-forced ovens, check the manufacturer's manual.

	°C (CELSIUS)	°F (FAHRENHEIT)	GAS MARK
Very slow	120	250	½
Slow	150	275 – 300	1 – 2
Moderately slow	160	325	3
Moderate	180	350 – 375	4 – 5
Moderately hot	200	400	6
Hot	220	425 – 450	7 – 8
Very hot	240	475	9

index

Are you missing some of the world's favourite cookbooks?

The Australian Women's Weekly cookbooks are available from bookshops, cookshops, supermarkets and other stores all over the world. You can also buy direct from the publisher, using the order form below.

MINI SERIES £3.50 190x138MM 64 PAGES

TITLE	QTY	TITLE	QTY	TITLE	QTY
4 Fast Ingredients		Fast Soup		Potatoes	
15-minute Feasts		Finger Food		Roast	
50 Fast Chicken Fillets		Gluten-free Cooking		Salads	
50 Fast Desserts		Healthy Everyday Food 4 Kids		Simple Slices	
After-work Stir-fries		Ice-creams & Sorbets		Simply Seafood	
Barbecue Chicken		Indian Cooking		Skinny Food	
Biscuits, Brownies & Biscotti		Indonesian Favourites		Spanish Favourites	
Bites		Italian Favourites		Stir-fries	
Bowl Food		Jams & Jellies		Summer Salads	
Burgers, Rösti & Fritters		Japanese Favourites		Tagines & Couscous	
Cafe Cakes		Kids Party Food		Tapas, Antipasto & Mezze	
Cafe Food		Last-minute Meals		Tarts	
Casseroles		Lebanese Cooking		Tex-Mex	
Casseroles & Curries		Low-Fat Delicious		Thai Favourites	
Char-grills & Barbecues		Low Fat Fast		The Fast Egg	
Cheesecakes, Pavlova & Trifles		Malaysian Favourites		The Packed Lunch	
Chinese Favourites		Mince		Vegetarian	
Chocolate Cakes		Mince Favourites		Vegie Main Meals	
Christmas Cakes & Puddings		Muffins		Vietnamese Favourites	
Cocktails		Noodles		Wok	
Crumbles & Bakes		Noodles & Stir-fries		Young Chef	
Cupcakes & Cookies		Outdoor Eating			
Curries		Party Food			
Dried Fruit & Nuts		Pickles and Chutneys			
Drinks		Pasta		TOTAL COST £	

Photocopy and complete coupon below

Name _____

Address _____

_____ Postcode _____

Country _____ Phone (business hours) _____

Email*(optional) _____

* By including your email address, you consent to receipt of any email regarding this magazine, and other emails which inform you of ACP's other publications, products, services and events, and to promote third party goods and services you may be interested in.

I enclose my cheque/money order for £ _____ or please charge £ _____

to my: ☐ Access ☐ Mastercard ☐ Visa ☐ Diners Club

Card number | | | | | | | | | | | | | | | | |

3 digit security code *(found on reverse of card)* _____

Cardholder's
signature _____ Expiry date ____ /____

To order: Mail or fax – photocopy or complete the order form above, and send your credit card details or cheque payable to: Australian Consolidated Press (UK), 10 Scirocco Close, Moulton Park Office Village, Northampton NN3 6AP, phone (+44) (01) 604 642200, fax (+44) (01) 604 642300, e-mail books@acpuk.com or order online at www.acpuk.com
Non-UK residents: We accept the credit cards listed on the coupon, or cheques, drafts or International Money Orders payable in sterling and drawn on a UK bank. Credit card charges are at the exchange rate current at the time of payment.
All pricing current at time of going to press and subject to change/availability.
Postage and packing UK: Add £1.00 per order plus 75p per book.
Postage and packing overseas: Add £2.00 per order plus £1.50 per book. **Offer ends 31.12.2007**